S0-BTE-507

THE ILLUSTRATED
JOHN LENNON

GEOFFREY GIULIANO
BRENDA GIULIANO

JG PRESS

Copyright © Something Fishy Productions Ltd., 1993

Published in the USA 1996 by JG Press
Distributed by World Publications, Inc.

The JG Press imprint is a trademark of
JG Press, Inc.
455 Somerset Avenue
North Dighton, MA 02764

ISBN 1 57215 210 9

All rights reserved. No part of this publication may be reproduced, stored in a retrieval
system, or transmitted in any form or by any means, electronic, mechanical, photo-
copying, recording, or otherwise, without prior written permission of Something Fishy
Productions Ltd.

Every effort has been made to trace the ownership of all copyrighted material and to
secure permission from copyright holders. In the event of any question arising as to the
use of any material, we will be please to make the necessary corrections in future print-
ings.

Printed and bound in China

CONTENTS

DEDICATION

To Eddie 'The Walrus' Porter, for his many years of selfless devotion to the Beatles' elderly family members and the legion of unknown Beatle People around the world.

And, of course, to John.

Foremost amongst the tribulations of being uncle to one so famous as John Lennon is knowing how to accurately assess the impact of someone who, at the same time is an international hero and also simply, "Our John." To be sure, John possessed an almost magical talent, but I prefer to remember him as the lanky, good natured young boy who used to tease me about my rapidly receding hairline (hair being a very major part of the Lennon family fortune as you know) and goad me for not making it down to his place in Surrey often enough. Whenever I did find the time to visit, however, it was as if time stood still. Inside the privacy of his plush Tudor mansion it was all slaps on the back, silly evenings spent playing Scrabble and lovely long dinners together tucking into some very memorable Liverpool fryups.

Although John and his dad, Fred went through some relatively rough patches together I resisted ever getting myself in the middle and hence, was able to stay friends with both. That these two loved each other devoutly was never in question. Things just got off to rather a bumpy start between them early on and left a lot of scars. It's sad, of course, but it's not really too unheard of in families today is it?

As far as the long-standing public perception of my elder brother and indeed, the entire Lennon clan are concerned, I must tell you, how ever many books, magazines or newspapers you've

read over the years, the true story of John Lennon, the Beatles and his proud and accomplished family, has yet to see the light day. Of all the punters out there in the trenches, I must say that Geoffrey Giuliano so far out distances them all in his sterling commitment to accuracy, insight and detail as to leave all the other latter day Beatle pundits scratching around in the dust. To say that Geoffrey is the world's foremost authority on the Beatles is to subtlety understate, for my money (and I've read them all) Mr. Giuliano *is* Beatle literature.

Unlike any work ever relating to The Fab Four, The Illustrated John Lennon finally gives those who revered John a fitting record of his incredible life and times. That means quite a lot to me personally, as I'm sure it does to everyone who ever loved them.

Charles Lennon

New Years 1993, Liverpool, England

CHAPTER ONE

LITTLE BOY LOST

John and a friend back home in Liverpool

Jack Lennon, John's grandfather, had always looked forward to returning home to Liverpool to retire. Born in Dublin and raised in Liverpool, he spent many years in America as a founding member of the Kentucky Minstrels.

After working so long on the stage as a professional singer, dancer, and comedian, he finally returned home, a happy man. Soon after he had settled down in a comfortable, lower-middle-class neighbourhood on the outskirts of Liverpool's bustling city centre, his third son, Freddie, was born. Five years later, in 1917, Jack Lennon took sick and died suddenly, leaving the care of his three young sons - Charlie, Sidney, and Freddie - to Liverpool's Bluecoat Orphanage.

Freddie Lennon left the orphanage at fifteen and soon secured a respectable job as an office boy. A short time later, while sitting in Sefton Park on one of his numerous "unscheduled" afternoons off, he met Julia Stanley, a chatty, vivacious, good-natured schoolgirl whose father, George, was an officer with the Liverpool Salvage Company. Freddie and Julia went out together on and off for the next ten years, but certainly not with the blessings of the Stanleys, who considered themselves a definite cut above the careless, freewheeling, Lennon.

At sixteen Freddie signed on as a steward on a passenger ship in the White Star Line. Although the work was gruelling and tiresome, he enjoyed life at sea and quickly worked his way up to the responsible position of headwaiter in the posh dining hall of the luxurious ocean liner. On one of his infrequent shore leaves, against the wishes of Julia's family and without so much as a pound note between them, Freddie and Julia were married on December 3, 1938, at the public register office at 64 Mount Pleasant Road. The happy couple spent their honeymoon at the cinema, and the next day Freddie sailed away

to the West Indies for a three-month tour of duty.

A little under two years later, during another of her husband's extended stints abroad, a very pregnant Julia Lennon packed her tiny suitcase and checked into the Maternity Hospital in Oxford Street. Just after seven o'clock the next morning, on October 9, 1940, with Liverpool under heavy bombing from the Nazis, John Winston Lennon was born. He was immediately placed under his mother's sturdy iron bed to protect him in case the overcrowded hospital suffered a direct hit. Julia's sister Mimi (who later raised John) remem-

Schoolboy John as a Liverpool toddler

Lennon's boyhood home

bers, "The minute I saw John I was overjoyed. I went on and on about him, almost forgetting my poor sister."

John quickly grew into a very clever, dreamy little boy. His first recollection is of walking along the Pier Head with his Grandpa Stanley. He must have been wearing new shoes, he thinks, because he remembers his feet hurt so his grandpa slit the heels with a pocketknife, making them fit better. By the time John was three years old, Freddie and Julia had called it quits, and John went to live with his Auntie Mimi and Uncle George in Woolton. "Julia had met another man by the name of John Dykins," says Mimi. "Taking John would have been very difficult for her, so I offered to look after him myself. We had no children, and John was such a lovely, bright little child I couldn't bear to see him hurt. Both Fred and Julia wanted me to adopt him, but I could never get them both down to the office to sign the papers."

John's first school was Dovedale Primary. He was a cheerful boy, full of fun and mischief, who impressed both schoolmates and teachers with his natural leadership and naughty sense of adventure. He was also quite creative. By the age of seven he was even writing his own books. One of them, "Sport, Speed. Edited and Illustrated by J.W. Lennon," contained a witty collection of poems, caricatures, and short stories that hinted at his talent as a writer with a keen sense of the absurd.

When he was twelve, John left Dovedale for Quarry Bank Grammar School just a mile or so away from his aunt's house on Menlove Avenue. Then in June 1953 his beloved uncle George died unexpectedly from a massive haemorrhage caused by an undiscovered liver ailment. His death was a terrible blow to John. His aunt Mimi believes it was George's sudden death that strengthened John's early resolve to isolate himself emotionally from things too personal or painful for his sensitive, artistic psyche to handle.

John's years at Quarry Bank were characterised by the consistent academic failure and random creative achievement of a young man struggling with the seed of genius sown in the soil of middle-class conformity. He recalls his early frustration: "People like me are aware of their so-called genius even as a kid. Didn't they see that I was cleverer than anyone else in the school? And that the teachers were stupid, too? I used to say to me auntie, "You throw my bloody poetry out and you'll regret it when I'm famous," and she threw the stuff out! I never forgave her for not treating me like a genius when I was a child. Why didn't they train me? Why did they keep forcing me to be a cowboy like the rest of them? I was different, I was always different. Whey didn't anybody notice me?"

Shortly after the death of John's uncle George in 1953 his mother, Julia, re-entered his life. Although John heard very little about her whereabouts over the years, he had often wondered about her and secretly wished he could see her again. Then when he found out that she lived just a few short miles away in Allerton with her common-law husband, John Dykins (whom John preferred to call "Twitchy"), and

BEATLES COLOR CARDS

MEET JOHN LENNON
Vital Statistics:
Birthday—Oct. 9, 1940
Birthplace—Liverpool
Hair—Brown
Eyes—Brown
Height—5'11"
Weight—159
Favorite Color—Green
Favorite Food—Corn Flakes
Hobby—Writing
Favorite Singer—Shirelles
Likes—Cats
Favorite Type of Girl—His Wife
Brothers & Sisters—2 Step-Sisters

©T.C.G.   PRINTED IN U.S.A.

Bubbly Beatle John back in the bygone days of Beatlemania

their daughters, Julia and Jacqui, he was thrilled. John remembers: "I started cycling up to see her occasionally, and soon she became rather like a young auntie to me. As I grew older, I began to have some nasty rows with Mimi. So I used to run away and stay with Julia for the weekend or maybe a few weeks at a time." Julia encouraged John in whatever he wanted to do. But most of all it was Julia's knowledge of popular American music that turned on John and his pals. "I started off with a banjo at fifteen which my mother taught me how to play," says John. "My first guitar cost ten pounds. It was one of those advertised in the paper you sent away for. Julia got it for me. I remember it had a label on the inside which said, 'Guaranteed Not to Split.' My mother used to say she could play any stringed instrument there was, and she really did teach me quite a lot. The first tune I ever learned to play was *That'll Be The Day* by Buddy Holly.

In early 1956 John and his friends Eric Griffiths, Len Garry, Colin Hanton, Pete Shotton, and Rod Murray got together and formed a skiffle group they called the Quarry Men. Named in honour of Quarry Bank Grammar School, the group played its first gig at the annual Empire Day celebrations on Rosebury Street. The boys played from the back of an open lorry and were paid nothing. But the day went well, and soon the Quarry Men were appearing regularly at local parties and weddings, but most of all just for fun.

Meanwhile, having long since swapped the old trumpet his dad had given him for a guitar, Paul McCartney was making progress. Always the perfectionist, he practiced everywhere – in the lavatory, in the bathtub, on the bus – even at school. A fellow classmate, Ian James, also took up the guitar, and soon the two were cycling around

Yet another boring interview

Opposite: **Standing to attention on the set of** *How I won the War*

Liverpool with their instruments strapped to their backs, looking for places to play. Much to Jim McCartney's dismay Paul had taken to wearing the sort of clothes a guitar-picking teddy boy might choose. With his long, slicked-back hair piled high over his forhead, narrow drainpipe trousers, and white, sparkly sports coat, he might even have managed to fool a few people! That is, if it wasn't for that perpetually innocent, choirboy face of his. At fourteen Paul McCartney was far from being a tough Liverpool teddy boy, but he was also a long way from being the proper schoolboy Jim McCartney would have preferred.

Ivan Vaughan, an old schoolmate of John's, had recently met and befriended Paul McCartney. On June 15, 1956, the two boys went together to see the Quarry Men perform at an outdoor party at the Woolton Parish Church. Paul was impressed with what he heard and remembers John singing the Del Vikings' *Come Go With Me*. "John didn't really know all the words, though, so he made up his own," says Paul. "It was something like 'Come on go with me, down to the penitentiary ....' I thought 'Wow, he's great. That's a good band there!'" After the performance Paul met the group in the church hall. He recalls his first encounter with John Lennon: "I played him *Twenty Flight Rock* and a few other tunes I'd learned. Then he played me all of his stuff, and I remember he seemed a little bit drunk. Quite a nice

On holiday with first wife Cynthia, 1965

chap, but he did smell rather beery."

About a week later Paul took a spin over to Menlove Avenue to visit Ivan. On the way home he happened to meet Pete Shotton, who informed him that John had been impressed with his guitar work and wouldn't mind if he wanted to join the group. "Sure, okay," said Paul. "Cheerio then, Pete." His first public performance with the Quarry Men was at a dance held at the Conservative Club in Broadway. After the dance was over, Paul played John a couple of numbers he'd written himself. One of them was called *I Lost My Little Girl*. Not to be out-done, John soon started thinking up his own tunes and bouncing them off Paul. And so began, very casually and with no apparent fuss, the greatest two-man songwriting partnership of this century.

George Harrison's initial interest in the guitar came about slowly. Mrs. Harrison remembers that one day she started finding sheets of paper covered with drawings of guitars among his school things. Soon afterward she bought George an old secondhand box guitar from one of his classmates for three pounds. "George tried very hard to teach himself to play," recalls his mother, "but progress was very slow and painful. I told him to just dig in and keep at it if he really wanted to learn. And by God, he did. Sometimes he'd sit up all night and practice until his fingers bled."

George's dedication to his music gradually paid off. As his fingers became increasingly nimble, he began putting together the simple, flowing rhythms that were to become his unique musical signature. In 1956 George formed his own group, the Rebels. With his brother Peter and Arthur Kelly on guitars and two other friends on the tea chest and mouth organ, they played a dance at the Speke British Legion Club for the whopping sum of ten bob each.

Talk of George's newfound musical accomplishment soon reached the ears of Paul McCartney, who would often go round to George's, lugging along his guitar for an impromptu jam session. Then in early 1958 Paul introduced George to the Quarry Men and, more important to music history, to John. "I listened to George play and asked him if he knew the song *Raunchy*," says John. "Well he did, and so I had to make the decision whether or not to let him in the group. Finally I said, 'Okay, you're in, mate.' And then it was really just the three of us from that day on."

By the time George became a bona fide member of the Quarry Men, things had begun to look up for the band, but personally John Lennon was undergoing difficult times. On July 15, 1958, his free-spirited mother was knocked down by a car and killed while crossing Menlove Avenue. "She got killed by an off-duty copper who had been drinking,"

Ripping it up with George on tour, 1964

Opposite: **At the end of a long day during the height of Beatlemania**

John recalls. "I was just sixteen at the time, so that was another big trauma for me. I lost her twice, and it made me very bitter. I cried a lot about not having her anymore, and it was torture. Still, being so much on my own at that age gave me a certain awareness of myself and a sense of independence I might not have otherwise developed."

Around this time John left his aunt's pleasant, decidedly middle-class home and moved into a very shabby one-room flat at 3 Gambier Terrace with his good friend Stuart Sutcliffe. John remembers his life there: "We lived rough all right. It was a dirty old flat. I think we spent about four months there, practicing and painting. It was just like a rubbish dump. The others tried to tidy it up a bit, but I didn't bother. I left all my gear there when we went to Hamburg."

John was now attending classes at the Liverpool College of Art and soon began playing occasional lunchtime sessions with his group, renamed the Silver Beatles, in the student lounge. After tiring of being known as the Quarrymen, the group had been briefly called Johnny and the Moondogs. John and Paul even performed a few gigs under the unlikely name of the Nurk Twins. Although John's friend Stuart was a talented artist, he had little appreciable musical ability, but that didn't stop John from inviting him to join the group. Besides; Stuart had just earned sixty pounds from the sale of one of his paintings and could afford to buy his own first-class bass guitar.

By this time the group had gone through a succession of different drummers and had finally settled on a quiet, strangely good-looking fellow from West Derby by the name of Pete Best. Pete was born in 1941, the oldest child of Mona and Johnny Best. His father, an ex-Liverpool boxing promoter, met his wife in her native India during the

Second World War. Pete was a good-natured but rather shy little boy who grew up to be an excellent student, easily passing five subjects at the O level and entering the Sixth Form near the end of his school days. "I got good and fed up with being at school as time went by," says Pete. "I'd been thinking of going on to teachers' training college but left just before sitting for my A levels. Paul McCartney, an old acquaintance, rang me out of the blue one day and asked me if I'd like to become their drummer and go to Hamburg with them. The pay was fifteen pounds a week, which was a lot of money in those days. Anyway, it was definitely much better than going to a training college for the rest of my life."

Allan Williams, an aggressive, fast-talking scouser with a keen eye for a fast buck, was the first real promoter to take an interest in the Silver Beatles. He liked the Boys personally and figured they might one day even have a shot at becoming professional. Acting on their behalf, he negotiated a deal for them to appear in Hamburg at Bruno Koschmeider's Indra Club. The Beatles played Hamburg twice during a short period - from August to December 1960 and from April to July 1961. George Harrison recalls: "In my opinion our peak for playing live was in Hamburg. You see, at that time we weren't so famous, and people who came to see us were drawn in simply by our music and

Opposite: **In New York, 1964**

Below left: **The Beatles entertaining the troops**

Below right: **A rare shot of John playing keyboards**

Above: **John during the filming of the Beatles' second feature,** *Help*

Below: **High stepping John acting in** *A Hard Day's Night*

whatever atmosphere we managed to create. We got very tight as a band there, as most nights we had to play for over eight hours. We were at four different clubs altogether in Germany. Originally we played the Indra, and when that was shut down, we went over to the Kaiserkeller and then later on to the Top Ten. That was a fantastic place, probably the best one on the Reeperbahn. There was even a sort of natural echo on the microphones - it was really a gas. The Star Club was very rough, but we enjoyed ourselves there as well. We developed quite a big repertoire of our own songs but still played mainly old rock 'n' roll tunes. Back in England all the bands were getting into wearing matching ties and handkerchiefs and were doing little dance routines like the Shadows. We were definitely not into that bit, so we just kept on doing what we felt like, and ultimately I guess it worked out okay."

If the Beatles' music underwent a powerful, positive transformation in Hamburg, so did the boys themselves. Stuart met and fell fiercely in

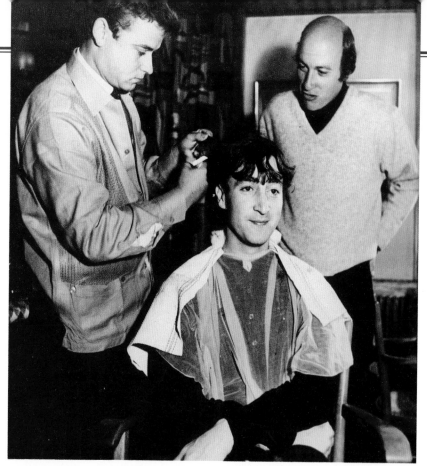

Right: Lennon takes a quick trim while movie director Richard Lester looks on

Below: On the set of the Beatles' first film

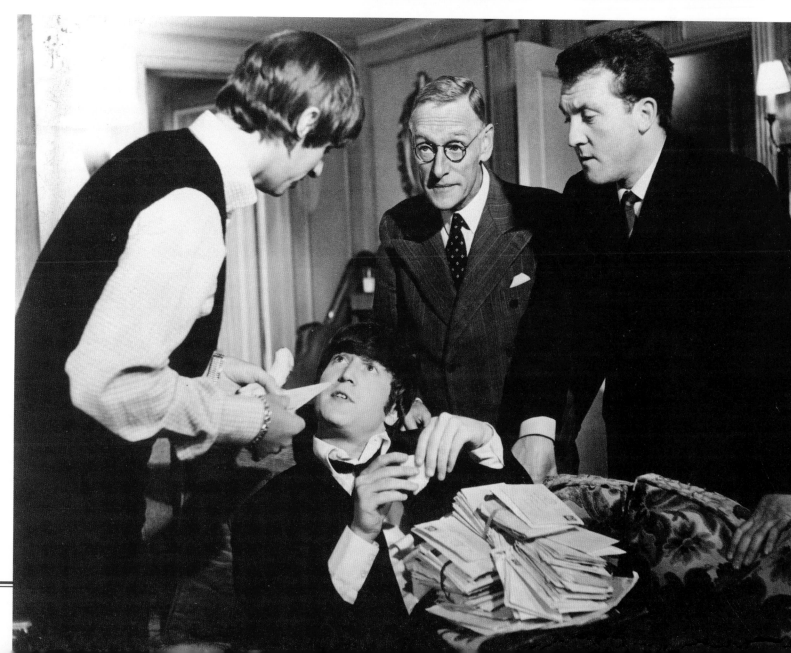

Above: **Visiting a long lost relative in New Zealand**

Above: **John in late 1966**

Right: **As Muskateer Gripweed in the wonderful anti-war spoof,** *How I won the War.*

Main picture: **Beatling in America in the early days**

Above: **At the gala premiere of**
How I won the War

Below: **Busking with the Fab Four,
late 1965**

love with a beautiful German photographer named Astrid Kirchherr. She and two friends, illustrator Klaus Voorman and fellow photographer Jurgen Vollmer, were among the first from the artistic community to appreciate the potential that the Beatles' vibrant music and charismatic personalities might hold for a mass audience. Soon both Astrid and Jurgen were photographing the Beatles as a group and individually in various locations around the Reeperbahn.

Meanwhile John, Paul, George, and Pete were busy soaking up what they could of Hamburg's notorious nightlife. As well as sampling the strong German beer, they also became enamoured of an over-the-counter amphetamine called Prellys, which delivered an occasional burst of artifical energy to the overworked musicians and also gave them their first taste of the joys of illicit self-medication. On the Reeperbahn drugs were an easily obtained, two-bob, ten-hour vacation from a crazy world of unending sensory overload. The buxom, accommodating frauleins of the Grosse Freiheit also packed some surprises for the five basically naive scousers. Once, legend has it, while John was groping one of the more heavily made-up patrons of the Top Ten, he discovered to his horror that "she" was outfitted with an extra piece of decidedly unfeminine physiology. There were probably at

least one bloody nose, one very red face, and countless belly laughs among the boys over that little indiscretion!

Tony Sheridan, a popular, transplanted English singer with a large, faithful following among the Germans, was regarded by many as the "performer in residence" at the Top Ten, one of the best clubs in Germany. Because Tony was really a solo artist, he often used whatever band happened to be playing the club as his backing group. In April 1961, during the Beatles' second trip to Hamburg, Tony used them at Polydor recording sessions produced by the well-known German orchestra leader Berty Kaempfert. Although the Beatles had recorded a few times before, once as the Quarry Men in a Liverpool basement studio and then in the fall of 1960 at Akustik studios in Hamburg, these were their first professional sessions. They recorded eight tunes, six backing Tony and two others. *My Bonnie* and *Cry For A Shadow*. Years later these recordings became pivotal in a lawsuit brought by Tony Sheridan against the Beatles and Apple Records, but for now the sessions were an important milestone for the boys. No longer were they simply another scruffy rock band posing as professional; however rough and uneven the finished product may have been the Beatles had finally made a record!

Above left: **He's crazy. No he flipped!**

Above right: **Father Lennon blesses the multitudes, 1967**

CHAPTER TWO

A FINE NATURAL IMBALANCE

Arriving at yet another prestigious party

Opposite: At the premiere of the Beatles' animated hit, *Yellow Submarine*

Once it got going, Beatlemania swept across the British Isles with an intensity and momentum far beyond anything Brian Epstein or the Boys could have envisioned. It was hard to believe that when he first took over the Beatles, Brian had been unable to interest any of the major record labels and that it was only by the luckiest of coincidences that he landed a deal with Parlophone. Now everywhere the Beatles went, they were pursued by hordes of screaming, crying, swooning young women. And by a ruthless British press, who faithfully reported every successive outbreak of Beatlemania with the kind of coverage usually reserved for lesser news events, such as the outbreak of world war! Still the Beatles remained dissatisfied. Locked up by themselves for days on end in one lifeless hotel room after another, they talked of only one thing - conquering America!

Midway over the Atlantic on board Pan Am flight 101 to New York, the Beatles were feeling more than a little anxious about what sort of reception they would find on landing. But all doubts were swept away when at 1.35 on the afternoon of February 7, 1964, they touched down on the icy runway of Kennedy Airport. As the plane slowly made its way toward the terminal, the shrill sound of over ten thousand teenage voices chanting and screaming for the Beatles penetrated the hull of the aircraft. Peering out of the fozen windows of the DC-10, the Beatles saw for the first time what America had in store for the. "Every kid from Broadway to the Bronx was there," remembers one seasoned veteran of the quizzical New York press corps. "They were all wearing buttons that said 'I LIKE THE BEATLES' and waving banners and placards they'd made up at home. Little girls were fainting, cops were sticking bullets in their ears to help drown out the scream-

John

ing, and the poor Beatles were just standing there at the door of the plane completely and utterly in shock. No one, I mean no one, had ever seen or even remotely suspected anything like this!" The boys were led to the airport press lounge, where they held the largest, wildest press conference in the history of New York City. John Lennon yelled at everyone to shut up, and the entire room applauded! Beatlemania now held the entire world in its grasp as an untold number of hustlers, con men, and copycats all clamoured to jump on board the bandwagon.

After the press conference the Beatles were ceremoniously driven into New York City and installed in a palatial suite of rooms at the Plaza Hotel. George didn't like the food, but this didn't really bother the management, because it didn't especially care for the Beatles and their fifteen thousand or so screaming fans tearing up the hotel. This was rather ungraciously made known to the entire world by offering the Beatles to any other four-star hotel that would have them.

The fact that New York's innkeepers lacked a sense of humour, however, was no indication that the rest of the nation wasn't ready for a good, hearty "Yeah, yeah, yeah." Even Elvis Presley, the Beatles' rock

Opposite left: **Making a plea for peace in snowy Denmark**

Opposite right: **Although Yoko's talent was legend in the mind of her loving husband John, most of us, missed the point**

Below: **John, Paul, George and Billy? Drummer Nichols sits in for Ringo,1964.**

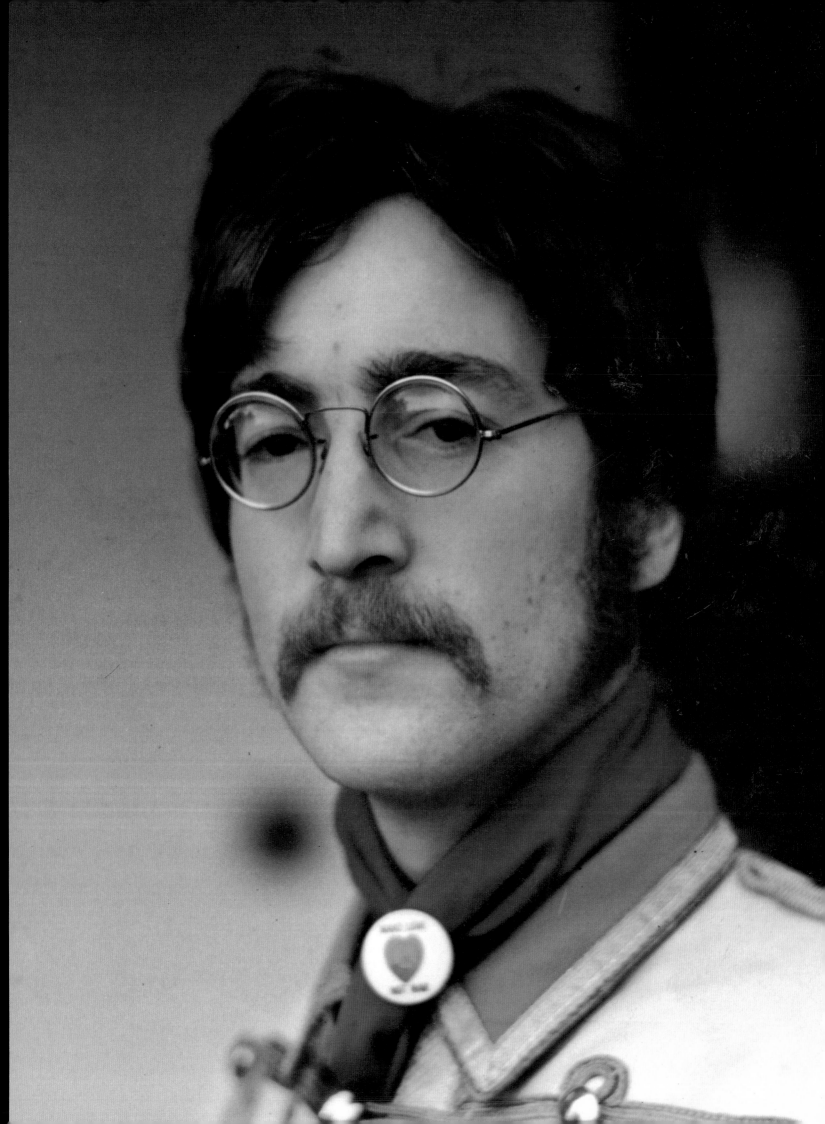

'n' roll hero, acknowledged their impact on the music scene by sending them a congratulatory telegram following their first appearance on the "Ed Sullivan Show." In fact, many newspapers were already calling for the "King" to abdicate his throne. The New York Daily News wrote, "The Presleyan gyrations and caterwauling of yesterday are but lukewarm dandelion tea in comparison to the 100-proof elixir served up by the Beatles." And so it seemed that John Lennon's longtime wish that the Beatles might one day be bigger than Elvis was finally coming true.

The Fab Four take a break in shooting for *The Magical Mystery Tour*

Despite their many triumphs, however, as the Beatles toured the United States the pattern of lunacy that constantly surrounded them began to take its toll. John and George, in particular, became very cynical about the fact that the Beatles seemed to have become an excuse for kids to run wild in the streets, smashing up phone boxes and climbing up elevator shafts in hopes of catching a brief glimpse of one of their idols. Plopped down in the middle of Anytown, U.S.A., the Fab Four were forced to perform in outdoor

Opposite:* In the studio during sessions for *Sergeant Pepper

***Right:* He *was* the Walrus**

sports arenas with virtually no acoustics, proper amplification, or adequate security. "The bigger we got, the more unreality we had to face," says John. "It was all just a bad joke to me. One has to completely humiliate oneself to be what the Beatles were. I didn't know, I couldn't foresee. It just happened gradually, bit by bit, until you're doing exactly what you don't want with people you simply can't stand! The people you hated when you were ten." Still the tours lumbered on, each city melting into the next, each performance more meaningless than the one before. Their ever-faithful road manager, Mal Evans, remembers they even faced being electrocuted by their own instruments when they were forced to continue performing at outdoor gigs when it began to rain. "What could we do?" he muses. "If we'd stopped the show, the kids would have stampeded and probably torn us limb from limb!" A plane carrying the Beatles was shot at by a jealous boyfriend, and Brian became the victim of an extortion attempt after a shadowy love affair with a New York construction worker. But what was worse - what made it absolutely impossible for the Beaatles to continue touring for an extended period of time - was the undeniable reality that in the midst of all this chaos, the audiences had forgotten the music. Everyone was still applauding, but no one was really listening anymore.

From February 2, 1963, to August 29, 1966, the Beatles played over 225 live shows in almost every country and continent of the free world. They performed for millions of hysterical teenyboppers, were pelted by rock-hard jelly beans, and were constantly harassed by fans looking for souvenirs - everything from personalised autographs to bits of their hair, clothes, and even fingernails. Crippled children were wheeled into the boys' dressing rooms in hopes that a dose of their mysterious power might restore or straighten lifeless limbs and twisted bodies. Airport terminals were continually soiled by young women who wet their pants on catching up with their favourite Beatle.

This was, all in all, quite a lot of madness for four provincial young men from the north of England to endure. And so, when the Beatles laid down their instruments after their last number at Candlestick Park in San Francisco in August 1966, they said good-bye to public performing forever. From now on John, Paul, George and Ringo would devote themselves exclusively to working their magic only in the privacy and sanctity of the recording studio.

The Beatles' retreat from public life into the studio gave them greater scope to express themselves musically and reduced the pressure of having to crank out one top-selling hit after another. After so many years of hustling to reach the top, the Beatles reveled in their newfound artistic freedom. One of the first and most significant manifestations of this change in direction was their concentrated effort to write better, more meaningful songs. John explains: "Beatlemusic is when we all get together, you know. Of course, we really don't write songs together that much anymore. Now it's just occasional bits, a line or two. We used to write a lot when we were touring, mainly out of sheer boredom. But today

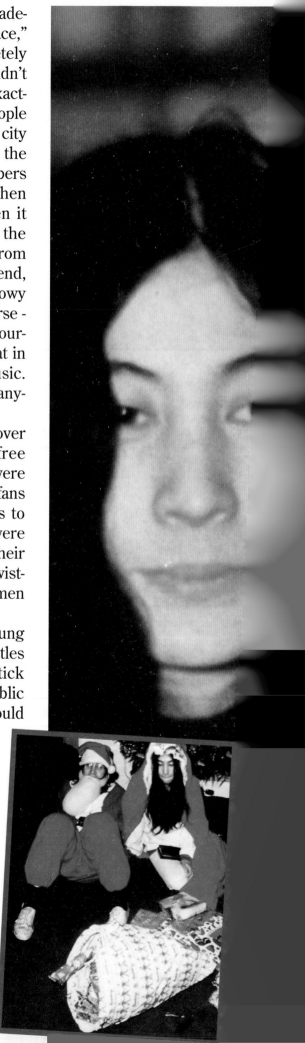

the Beatles just go into the studio, and it happens! See, I remember our early meetings with Dylan where he'd constantly go on about the words. Well, I naturally play with the lyrics anyway, but I suppose I made a more conscious effort to be 'wordy a la Dylan' after that. When I started out, you see, rock 'n' roll itself was the basic revolution to people of my age. We needed something loud and clear to break through all the unfeeling and repression that had been coming down on us kids. Rock makes good sense, but then again, so does pure sound. Paul has always said that in the end we'll all probably be writing one-note pop songs, and he's right. But for now we're still working with the concept of 'sound pictures' - that is, creating visual images through the medium of

Above: **Exiting Apple**
Right: **At the opening for Lennons' 'You Are Here' conceptual art exhibition,1968**

Previous page: **With young Julian at the Rolling Stones Rock and Roll Circus, 1969**
Inset: **Entertaining at the Apple Christmas party, 1968**

Opposite: **Lennon with a larger than life rendition of his birth certificate**

(Printed by Authority of the Register General)

Carefull COPY of an ENTRY of BIRTH

PERSUANT to the BIRTHS & DEATHS ACT

Registration District Liverpool in the County of Lancashire

B.CE...

...ing	NO.	When & Where Born	Sex	Signature of Informant	When Registered	Signature of Registrar	Name & Surname
...on	Nine	ninth October 1940 Oxford St Maternity Hospital. Liverpool	Boy	E Rigbr (X.S)	November 1940	K. Baue Whimp	Alfred Len...

...Whim Registrar of Births & Deaths for the District of Liverpool , in the County of Lancashire do hereby certify that the...

...of the entry No 7 in the Register of Births for the said district, and that such is now remaining in my Custody.

...s Hand this 27th day of November 1940

K. Baue Whim

REGISTRAR of BIRTHS & DE...

sound. There's still a lot to be learned in this area as well."

Albums like *Rubber Soul* and *Revolver* certainly shook up the Beatles' musical image with their innovate use of classical orchestrations, lofty, intricate lyrics, and the virtually unheard-of addition to popular music of sound effects. And although they were all very successful, they were little more than brief, though thoroughly engrossing, sideshows to the main event, *Sgt. Pepper's Lonely Hearts Club Band.*

The album was recorded with great enthusiasm at the EMI studios between December 1966 and April 1967. The project started off with the recording of *When I'm Sixty-Four* on December 10. Written chiefly by Paul, it also featured him on lead vocals, piano, and bass. Strongly influenced by the old-time music hall sounds of English vaudeville, this song typifies the extended repertoire the Beatles had worked to develop. The second tune committed to tape, the epic *A Day In The Life,* was initiated on January 19. Using a forty-one-piece orchestra and backed by a dreamy montage of vocal harmonies by John, Paul, and George, it is the longest song on the album, clocking in at five minutes, three seconds.

John and Paul recall the inspiration for the work. "I was writing the song with the 'Daily Mail' propped up in front of me on the piano," says John. "I had it open at the 'News in Brief' section or whatever they call it. Anyway, there was a paragraph about four thousand holes in Blackburn, Lancashire, being discovered, and there was still one word missing in that particular verse when we began to record. I knew the line should go, 'Now they know how many holes it takes to ...the Albert Hall.' It was a nonsense verse really, but for some reason I just couldn't think of the bloody verb! What did the holes do to the

Below left: **Backstage at Toronto's Varsity Stadium where the newly formed Plastic Ono Band played to capacity crowds, 1969**

Below and right: **The radical left's white knights in action**

Albert Hall? It was actually Terry Doran who finally said, 'Fill the Albert Hall, John.'" Paul McCartney remembers: "There'd been a story about a lucky man who'd made the grade, and there was a photograph of him sitting in his big car, and when John saw it he just had to laugh! That's all just a little black comedy, you know. The next bit was another song altogether, but it happened to fit well with the first section. It was really only me remembering what it was like to run up the road to catch the school bus, having a smoke, and then going into class. We decided, 'Bugger this, we're going to write a real turn-on song!' This was the only one in the album written as a deliberate provocation to people. But what we really wanted was to turn you on the the truth rather than just bloddy pot!"

Another remarkable tune on the album is George's *Within You Without You*. Recorded in mid-March, the basic tracks

The Lennons stage their now famous 'Bed-In For Peace' at a posh Montreal hotel, 1969

Partying in London following a gig to promote the Lennons' *War is Over* poster campaign

In Montreux, 1969 to attend the Golden Rose Television Contest in which their film *The Rape* was entered

Main picture: Peace and Love baby!

Peace and Love, Baby!

were done by George with a little help from Neil Aspinall on the bamboura. Indian session musicians were brought in to play the exoctic dilruba, sword mandel, sitar, and tablas. George Martin helped out as overall producer-arranger as well as conducting and co-ordinating the eight violinists and three cellists brought in to add texture and mood to the track. George remembers how it all got started: "Klaus Voorman had a harmonium in his house, which I hadn't played before. I was doodling on it, playing to amuse myself, when 'Within You' started to come. The tune came initially, and then I got the first line. It came out of what we'd been discussing that evening.

The other ten songs on the album - *Lucy In The Sky With Diamonds, Sgt. Pepper's Lonely Hearts Club Band, With A Little Help From My Friends, Being For The Benefit Of Mr. Kite, She's Leaving Home, Fixing A Hole, Getting Better, Good Morning, Good Morning, Lovely Rita,* and the *Sgt. Pepper Reprise* - were all exquisitely crafted, as compelling and ingenious in their lyrical inspiration as they were revolutionary in style and innovative in production techniques.

The trendy, elaborate uniforms made for the "Pepper band" were the creation of the well-known London theatrical costumers, Bermans, with more than a little input from the Beatles themselves. At first the boys were going to dress in ordinary Salvation Army-style outfits, but when one of the tailors from the agency dropped by the studio with some fabric for them to examine, the Beatles immediately chose the brightest patterns from a pile of satin samples. Four pairs of outrageous orange and yellow patent leather shoes were ordered, and arrangements were made for John, Paul, George and Ringo to nip into Bermans to be measured and fitted for their costumes.

There they sifted through mountains of frogs, braids, medals, hats, and trinkets to find just the right accents for their pseudomilitary fantasy. Finally, the instruments the Beatles would hold on the cover were hired and collected by Mal Evans, who spent over four hours polishing them in preparation for the photo shoot. The montage of famous faces and figures forming the backdrop for the band was assembled by Peter Blake and Jann Haworth and photographed by Michael Cooper. This was a gargantuan task in itself and took months of painstaking work. Moreover, the plain, white paper sleeve that normally holds the record was replaced by a swirling red-and-wine-coloured inner wrapper designed and executed by a trio of Dutch designers called the Fool. *Sgt. Pepper's Lonely Hearts Club Band* was released on June 1, 1967, to a flood of acclaim from just about everyone who owned a record player. And it still stands today as the Beatles' crowning achievement; from then on rock, 'n' roll was no longer just teenage dance music - it was art.

The idea for Magical Mystery Tour, the Beatles' first TV movie, was conceived by Paul McCartney, and filming began on September 11, 1967. (It would have been produced sooner, but the Beatles' participation in the global satellite telecast "Our World" caused a delay.) The concept was quite simple - the Beatles would invite a select group of close friends, fan club secretaries, character actors, midgets, and cir-

Previous page: **John Lennon, Peace politician, 1969**

Opposite: **Lennon just after the tempestuous break-up of the Beatles**

Happy together

cus freaks to travel around the English countryside with them in a rented coach and just see what happened. Ringo, listed in the credits as "Richard Starkey MBE," was ostensibly director of photography, and although all the Beatles contributed to the final edting of the film, it was Ringo and Paul who looked after the overall production. Unfortunately, the film was not very well received by either the critics or the public after its premiere on BBC-1 on Boxing Day 1967. The London 'Daily Mail' called it "blatant rubbish," while the 'Los Angeles Times' reported, "Critics and Viewers Boo: Beatles Produce First Flop with Yule Film." Paul McCartney was definitely not amused and quite rightly commented that if the film had been shown in colour as originally intended, rather than black and white, it might have made more sense. Nevertheless, American network officials cancelled their option to broadcast the film in the United States. It is interesting to note, however, that today the film has attained cult status among collectors and is heavily traded on video cassette on the underground market.

But public acceptance of the film's soundtrack was a different matter. Released in England as a deluxe double EP (complete with a lovely, twenty-four page souvenir booklet) and in America as a straight twelve-inch LP, it immediately went straight to number one in both countries. Six tunes were written especially for the project - *Magical*

Watching Bob Dylan at the Isle of Wight Festival, 1969

Mystery Tour, The Fool On The Hill, Flying, Blue Jay Way, Your Mother Should Know, and *I Am The Walrus.* In the United States, West Germany, and a few other countries five "filler" tracks were added to round out the album - *Hello Goodbye, Strawberry Fields Forever, Penny Lane, Baby, You're A Rich Man,* and *All You Need Is Love.*

The Beatles' famous *White* album, released on November 22, 1968, was the first official group project to be released on their newly formed Apple Records. Recorded under the working title of "A Doll's House," it featured a stark, all-white cover designed by artist John Kosh with the title, "The Beatles," embossed on the front and an edition number stamped in grey ink just below. Inserted inside the double album were four 8" x 10" head shots of the Boys and a freaky, collage-style poster (that doubled as a lyric sheet) by Richard Hamilton. Most of the thirty-odd tracks were written during the Beatles' stay with the Maharishi Mahesh Yogi in early 1968, when they were still in their transcendental meditation phase. This album showed just how far the Beatles' widely diverse songwriting ability and increasing prowess in the studio had developed, as evidenced by two prominent tunes, *Glass Onion* and *Happiness Is A Warm Gun,* both written by John.

He remembers their inception: With *Glass Onion* I was just having a laugh, because there had been so much gobbledygook written about 'Sgt. Pepper'. People were saying, "Play it backwards while standing

Opposite: **John was always terrific with the fans. Here he is happily signing away at a New York theatre in 1976**

on your head and you'll get a secret message, etc. Why, just the other day I saw Mel Torme on TV saying that several of my songs were written to promote the use of drugs, but really, none of them were at all. So this one was just my way of saying, 'You're all full of shit!" As for *Happiness Is A Warm Gun*, I consider it one of my best. It's a beautiful song, and I really like all the things that are happening in it. It was put together from bits of about three different songs and just seemed to run the gamut of many types of music. I pulled the title straight off the cover of a gun magazine George Martin showed me. I thought, 'What a fantastic, insane thing to say.' A warm gun means you've just shot something."

By now faint cracks were beginning to show in the Beatles' inner circle. John and Paul were often at odds over problems arising in the studio, and Ringo and George were getting fed up with a lot of the nonsense that went with being a Beatle. Still, fans the world over thought

John and Yoko, rock 'n' roll's psychedelic, loving couple

Opposite: **Performing with a two-faced colleague on a TV special dedicated to British showbiz mogul Sir**

A timely message from Yoko during a 1970 appearance on Top of the Pops

Opposite: **The world's unlikeliest twins arrive in London after a late night flight**

Following pages: **Three views of John after shaving off his famous locks, 1970**

the *White* album was great and pushed it to the very top of the charts.

Yellow Submarine, the soundtrack album of their animated feature film and released on January 17, 1969, contained only four "new" songs - *Hey Bulldog*, *Only A Northern Song*, *It's All Too Much*, and Paul's rather thinly veiled plea for greater unity within the group, *All Together Now*. This recording project, while reasonably popular with fans, wasn't really much fun for the Beatles. John has said he found it embarrassing to be working on something as "lightweight" and "poppy" as *Hey Bulldog* during Yoko's first visits to the studio to watch him record. His personal standards about what tunes he would allow himself to do were very strict, and this song was only borderline material at best. Conversely, George's two contributions to the album, *Only A Northern Song* and *It's All Too Much*, were both strong, striking tunes, heavily introspective and deeply engrossing in their spacey, mantra-like melodies.

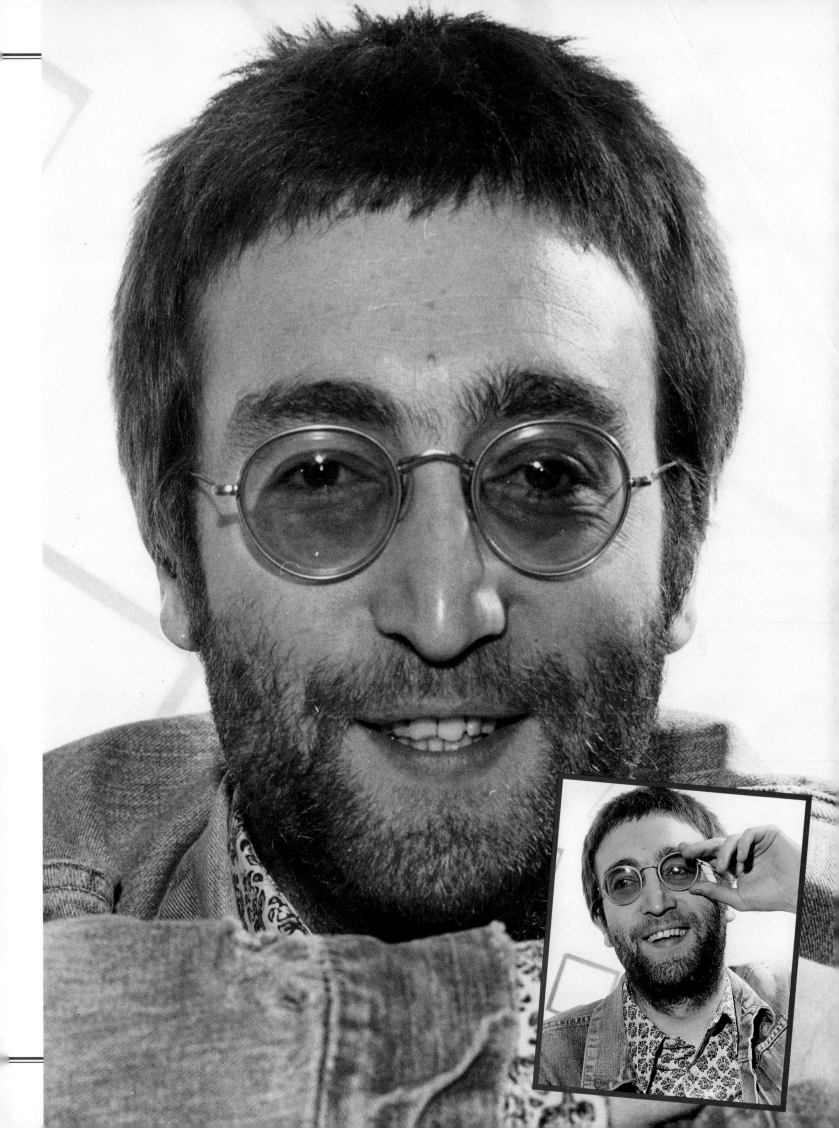

Following a press conference in the Jutland region of Denmark, 1970

Two other previously released recordings were added to the package to further emphasise the movie's swinging, upbeat message: *All You Need Is Love* and of course the wild undersea fantasy sung by Ringo, *Yellow Submarine*. Side two, an entertaining medley of incidental music from the film, was composed by George Martin and performed by his own orchestra. However, the album climbed to only number four in the Melody Maker charts and didn't really do much better in America.

Let It Be, originally called *Get Back*, was the Beatles' last official release as a group. Designed as a way to help them return to their original rock 'n' roll roots, it was promoted as a "new-phase Beatle album," but the truth was, it was their last hurrah. By the time the sessions for *Abbey Road* rolled around six months later, they had all but decided to go their separate ways.

John remembers: "In a nutshell, it was getting to be time for another Beatles movie or something, so Paul thought up the idea of us just playing live somewhere and then filming it, raw, as it happened, with no icing on top. But where? Someone mentioned the Colosseum in Rome, and I think originally Paul might have even suggested a bloody boat in the middle of the ocean. As for me, I was rapidly warming up to the idea of an asylum! He also had the mistaken impression that he was going to rehearse us. Of course by that time we'd been playing together for about twenty years or something, and we just couldn't get

George, John and Yoko during sessions for Lennon's landmark *Imagine* LP

Below left: Power to the People!

Below right: At Apple, 1970

into it. So anyway, we laid down a few tracks, but nobody was really into it at all. It was just such a very, very dreadful feeling being there in Twickenham Studios at eight o'clock in the morning with some old geezer pointing a camera up your nose expecting you to make good music with coloured lights flashing on and off in your face all the time. To me the whole thing ended up looking and sounding like a goddam bootleg version of an eight-millimeter home movie, so I didn't want to know about it. None of us did." George later declared, "I couldn't stand it! I decided, this is it! It's just not fun anymore; as a matter of fact, it's very unhappy being in this band at all!"

Strolling in front of the Dakota very close to the spot where John was brutally murdered

CHAPTER THREE

THE DREAMWEAVER

For John Lennon it was Brian Epstein's untimely death that precipitated the Beatles' breakup . "After Brian died we virtually collapsed," said John at the time. "Paul took us over, and supposedly led us, but we only went round in circles. As far as I'm concerned, that's when we really broke up."

For Paul, George, and Ringo, however, it may have been Yoko Ono's dramatic appearance on the scene that put the final nail into the group's coffin. Before Yoko no one had been able to penetrate the inner defences of the four brotherly musicians, but Yoko's clear-cut ambition to succeed with her art and be with her man broke those defences down.

Ringo, too, sorts out what was behind the breakup: "Because I left, because George left, because Yoko came in, because John left, because of the Apple business, because suddenly we all had individual things to do – millions of things. They're all part of it, you know. Little niggly things that cropped up because we'd been together for the past ten years and now wanted to do a few different things."

Another big problem for the Boys was the rapid disintegration of their multi-million-pound Apple empire and the inevitable squabbles that ensued over how to manage it properly after Brian died. Paul wanted to bring in his father-in-law, New York music-business attorney Lee Eastman, to help straighten things out, whereas John and the others were leaning toward hiring the Rolling Stones' manager, Allen Klein. Klein, a self-made music-publishing millionaire-turned-business-manager, was well known in American showbiz circles for being an extremely shrewd negotiator as well as a clever organiser. More important to the class-conscious Lennon, however, was the fact that Klein hailed from a working-class background and never pretended to

Counter-culture politicians, John and Yoko

Party time. John and Yoko at a Regine dinner party in New York, 1977

on going until Yoko was pregnant. What had you planned on doing in Biafra if you had (gone)?

John: We had an invitation from somebody connected with Biafra, and they wanted us to just go there and film. Publicity is what they want for their side of the story, and for it to come from somebody that isn't particularly politically one side or the other, somebody independent who can go there, see it, and come out again. That was the idea behind it.

Question: Can I ask you a question about the Beatles – do you ever expect to perform again? I know you had a bit of a hangup not wanting to.

John: It's like a few months ago George didn't. Now he's just been on tour with Bonnie and Delaney and Eric Clapton. I go off it and on it. And so there's four of us, you know, and I don't know how Ringo feels about it now, but I'm gonna try and sew him up for July, you know.

Question: What about the future of the Beatles – do you expect to remain as a foursome?

John: I've no idea. If we are comfortable, and enjoy being the Beatles, we'll do it - and when we don't we won't. That's always been the case. The last four years, every time we've made a record, it's been a decision of whether to carry it on from there. The point is, in the old days, Paul and I would knock off an LP and write most of the songs and do it. And nowadays there's three of us writing equally good songs, wanting that much space. The problem now is do you make a double album every time, which takes six months of your life, or do you make one album? We spend three or four months making one album, maybe get

two or three tracks each, that's the problem. You know, it's just a physical problem, and whether we do it or not I've no idea.

Question: Do you ever fear that your name coupled with the word "peace" could be used for other means?

John: There is always a danger of that, you know. But if anybody tries to use us, we have you people there; and if we find out, we'll say, "That rnan used us" you know, and that's our only protection against being used, is to tell you lot.

Question: Are there any circumstances in which you personally could support a war?

John: No.

Question: I'm wondering what your attitude would've been, for example, you're younger than I am...

John: Yeah, in 1939. I can only say don't talk to me about '39, talk to me about 1930.

Question: But the death of six million Jews in itself is not...

Yoko: But it was the responsibility of everybody.

John: It was all our responsbility, it wasn't like the Germans. I mean the Germans say "Oh, it was Hitler," and the world says, "Oh, it was the Germans," etc. etc. It was all our responsibility then. I know for people that were there then and all that – I was only a child being bombed and all that – it is different. But I just don't beleive it, you know. I believe it was all our repsonsibility before it happened, you know. That's all I can say about it. I don't believe in killing – whatever.

Lennon holds forth at a late night recording session, 1967

Question: How seriously do you consider the possibility that in your pursuit for peace that your manner of clothing and your hair would alienate more people than it would ever convince to come over to your side?

John: Yes, I understand that. Many people say "Why don't you get a butch haircut and a suit?" And the thing is, that's what politicians do. I try and be as natural as I can be under the circumstances. Now how many of the public are gullible to politicians with the nice picture of the family, the dog, and a whore on the side, church on Sunday. Now I could do that – I don't think people would believe it, you know. That is the politicians' way – youth certainly doesn't beleive it anymore. We have an intuition about "leaving one gate open." There's an old Chinese saying that "the castle falls from within." Say like America – no Communists are going to overrun 'em, the place'll collapse from inside. And always to leave one door open: if you have every door shut in the castle, the enemy'll attack from every side, and you stand a chance of losing. If you leave one door open, they'll concentrate there. Our door is hair, or mentioning irrelevancy to distract so as the attack doesn't hit us. And we try and be natural, you know. If I feel like cutting it, I'll cut it.

Question: We've heard a great deal about hidden significance in some of your records – you know this thing where if you play a certain record backwards it says "Turn me on, dead man" – is there anything to this?

John: No, all those things are beyond me, you know– I beleive that any...like, with this cigarette packet, you can read something into that if you want and nobody sees the same picture and all lyrics mean everything people want. But there was never any spe-cific "turn me on dead man," or the other famous one that I won't repeat, where you played it backward and got a secret message. If it's imagery it's imagery, if it's straight lyrics it's straight lyrics. But of course you can read anything into anything, that's why there's so many versions of the Bible.

Question: How did the death rumour about Paul get started?

John: I have no idea. I'm now being credited as the creator of a great publicity campaign for the Beatles. Now, if I'd thought of that idea, I don't know how I would've put it into action, and whether I would've done it or not, I don't know. I don't know how it started – it started, seems to me, the same way as the guy that resurrected my comment. about Jesus and got publicity for himself and his station and it just got out of his hands. I think it's the same kind of thing, somebody just...I don't know, I can't under-stand it myself.

Question: Do you think you will have more power reaching the new generation through a peace movement than trying to change the grown-up people's minds?

John: Yes, we're aiming at youth; our hope is with youth, you know. Because they will be the Establishment.

Yoko: The old people will come around too, if all the young are watching. Say if there's a Hitler in this world, somewhere in this world, now, we're hoping that this time we can stop him from doing something, because all the youth is watching, you know. And it's very difficult for Hitler to operate.

Question: John, you are now endowed with more influence over young people in the world than all the bishops and rabbis and priests put together. That is true. Do you ever feel any sense

The Lennons attend a premiere of Merce Cunningham's dance company in New York, 1977

John Lennon, the conscience of a generation

of...almost of fright, at the power that you have?

John: It's an abstract power, you know. It's like if we have something specific we'd like to use the power for – say we wanted to plug a certain product that wasn't peace, and I contact any press I know and try to get it over – there's a good chance it won't work. So I haven't got a power that I can really get hold of and do something with.

Question: But you're using it now for peace, and I think the whole world should be very grateful to you and Yoko for doing it. (Applause)

John: Well, thank you for that, you know.

Question: At the same time, do you not feel obligated to carry this message to Russia and China?

John: Sure, sure. We believe you start with two people, like in your own village, and our village happens to be the West. And of course we want to go to Russia and Czechoslovakia. We have to decide how we go and what we go as, you know. They don't really know much about us there. Do we just get on a train and arrive in Moscow as tourists, or do we try and take this Peace Festival I think that might be a good way. But the world is quite large still, and we've got to sort of get a good team going here first, and then when we're a bit more organized maybe we can go over there. I'd like to go somewhere over there, so as to stop that question arising again, before the end of '70, you know. I think there's a chance we might go to Czechoslovakia, and there's a good chance we can take this Peace Festival to Russia, I think. I believe they might allow pop stars to sing and play now. And I've heard it's easier to get in there than the States!

Question: Have you ever considered making a financial request to the Establishment? For example, a man like Henry Ford II?

John: Sure, sure. When we get a bit more organized. See what. we didn't want to do was become leaders. I believe in that Wilhelm Reich guy who says "don't be a leader," you know. We don't want to be the person people say "It was your fault we didn't get peace" or "It was your fault this happened." We want to be part of it, like people said "The Beatles were the movement". The Beatles were only ever part of a movement: we were influenced as much as we influenced. And John and Yoko refuse to be the leaders of the youth movement for peace.

Yoko: That's dictatorship.

John: That's dictatorship, you know. We want everybody to help us, we're just saying, "Listen, this is our flag, it's a white flag. Anybody else in the game?" And then if we can get something together...it takes time for this sort of news to get through to, say, Henry Ford or Onassis or somebody like that, because they'll be reading last year's papers or whatever, or the financial pages. They probably still think I'm on tour with Paul or something like that. When we get. something functional and organized, and a few people that aren't just John and Yoko, like Rabbi here and a few others... if you don't mind me calling you "straights," you know...we can approach from that angle and say, "Listen, man –we've got so much money, will you double it?" 'Cause we know they all do charity things.

Question: The point is, you won't call them this trip over?

John: Not this trip over, but of course I think of that. there's a lot of money around.

Question: Do you believe in God?

John: Yes. I believe that God is like a powerhouse, like where you keep electricity – a power station, and that He's a supreme power, but He's neither good nor bad nor left, right, or black or white. He just is, and that we tap that source of power and make of it what we will. Like electricity – you can kill people in a chair or you can light the room with it. I think God is.

Yoko: Also, we talk about having a belief in youth, you know, but youth includes everybody that is youthful, naturally. Then this voice said, "Well, what can we do?" and this question was always coming up, even when we had the Bed In in Montreal and all that. But just imagine what's happeniing now. For instance, maybe it was twisted around a little by reporters, but the Woodstock Festival or the Isle of Wight Festival, those were festivals with thousands and thousands of people, and there wasn't any violence. Maybe there were some mishaps, but no real violence. And that's fantastic – it's very historical because before that, when that number of people gathered it was only for war, or something violent. If it were for war even, the reasons why people were quiet was because maybe the colonel or major or something were telling them to be quiet! We were at the Isle of Wight and it was beautiful! That's starting to happen now, and all we can do is gather and show that we're very quiet, and show the noisy people, the violent people, to just make them ashamed to be violent.

John: Right.

Question: It's been said that Jesus Christ made the mistake of trying to save the whole world as one man. Do you think this, and is this why you don't believe in leadership?

John: I don't know about that – I just believe that leaders and father figures are the mistake of all the generations before us, and we can't rely on Nixon or on Jesus or whoever we tend to rely on. It's just a lack of responsibility that you expect somebody else to do it. It's "Oh, he must help me, and if he doesn't help me we kill him, or vote him out." I think that's the mistake – just having father figures. As long as we keep moving about, we will never be leaders.

Yoko: And you're the leader, you know. Everybody in this room has to lead the next world.

John: It's just that, you know. The Beatles were never leaders, but people imagined they were and now they're finding out, you know. And I won't be a leader, and leaders are just. "Okay, I will be then," and they have the badge on. Well, I'm not doing that.

Question: Could you give us your personal definition of peace?

John: Peace? Just no violence, and everybody grooving, if you don't mind me using the word. We've been invited by some guy to Rochester Cathedral, to do a two day fast over the 24th and 25th, so we're going with him, you know. We have a hard time making people think we mean what we say in Britain. It's like your parents, trying to say, "Look, I want my hair long."

Question: Do you remember the Cavern?

John: Yes.

Question: Do you think the kids are really as interested in peace as they were in the olden days?

John: Well, I don't know what they were interested in at the Cavern.

Yoko: I think they're getting to be very interested.

John: We consider this like we're in the Cavern now, we're in that stage – we haven't got out of Liverpool yet with this campaign, and we've got to break London and then America, you know, it's like that – I feel exactly the same as I did then about the Beatles as I do about peace and what we're doing now, you know. I don't care how long it takes, and what obstacles there are. We won't stop, you know.

Question: Is there any one incident that got you started on this peace campaign?

John: It built up over a number of years – but the thing that struck it off was we got a letter from a guy called Peter Watkins who made a film called "The War Game," and it was a long letter stating what's happening: How the media is controlled, how it's all run, everything that everybody knows, that bit. But he said it in black and white, for hours and hours on pages and it ended up "What are you going to do about it?" He said "People in your position and our position"...'cause he's a filmmaker "have a responsibility especially to use the media for world peace." And we sat on the letter for three weeks thinking, "Well, we're doing our best"...you know, "All you need is love," man, and all that...but finally we came up with the Bed Event after that, and that's what sort of sparked it off, you know. It was like getting your call-up papers for peace. We got it, and we sat on it for three weeks while we worked out what to do, and then we did the Bed Event.

Question: Is there any significance to these black clothes you're wearing?

John: We just like 'em, you know. We like black and white. And they're warm.

Question: What about Biafra?

John: Well, you know what we think about Biafra. We want to try to make Britain aware of its responsibility in Biafra, and that's what we're about, you know.

Question: Mrs. Lennon, one reads in the newspapers that your own home country of Japan is building up a certain industrial military capacity. Is this so, and what do you think about it?

Yoko: Well, we're doing something in Japan too, and it's a surprise. I'm sure that you'll hear it maybe in a week or so.

Question: You and your husband will do doing something?

Yoko: We're doing something now at this moment.

John: By remote control.

JOHN & YOKO
Toronto, December 1969

Opposite: John's last ever live performance with Elton John in New York

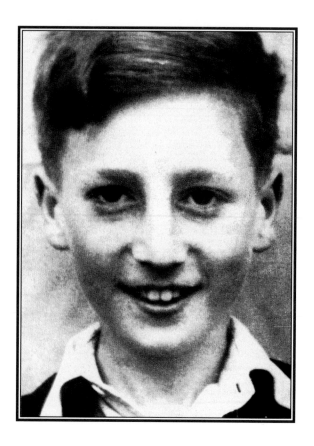

26 October 1855 John Lennon Sr., John's paternal grandfather (known throughout his life as 'Jack'), is born in Liverpool. He later became a founding member of the famous American travelling musical troupe, 'The Kentucky Minstrels.'

22 August 1874 George Ernest Stanley, stern patriarch of John's mother's family, is born at 120 Salisbury Street in Everton. He spent many years at sea, later coming ashore to work as an insurance investigator for the Liverpool Salvage Company.

14 December 1912 Alfred ('Alf') Lennon, John's seafaring father, is born at 27 Copperfield Street, Toxteth Park, Liverpool. His mother, Mary Maguire, was to bear two more sons, Charles and Stanley.

12 March 1914 Julia Stanley, mother to John Lennon, Victora Stanley, Julia and Jacqui Dykins, is born in Liverpool to Annie Millward and George Stanley.

1916 John Albert Dykins, Julia's common-law husband and the father of their two girls, Julia and Jacqui, is born.

August 1917 John Lennon Sr. dies of a liver disease at the age of sixty-one, thus leaving his three sons in the custodial care of Liverpool's Bluecoat Orphanage.

18 February 1933 Yoko Ono is born into the family of a wealthy Tokyo banker.

3 December 1938 Despite strong objections from the Stanleys, Alf Lennon marries the free-spirited young Julia at the Liverpool Register Office. Immediately after the austere civil ceremony, each of them returns to their own home. Three days later, Lennon signs on for a three-month tour of duty aboard a cargo ship bound for the West Indies.

10 September 1939 John's first wife, Cynthia Powell, is born in Blackpool.

23 June 1940 Stuart Sutcliffe is born in Edinburgh.

7 July 1940 Richard ('Ringo') Starkey is born to parents Richard and Elsie at 24 Admiral Grove, the Dingle, Liverpool.

9 October 1940 John Winston Lennon enters this world during a

German air-raid over Liverpool at 7 o'clock in the morning. Shortly after his birth he is placed under his mother's sturdy iron bed at the Liverpool Maternity Hospital. He is called John after his grandfather and Winston in honour of the Prime Minister, Winston Churchill. Once again his father Alf is away at sea.

24 November 1941 Randolph Peter Best, the Beatles' first really professional drummer, is born in Madras, India.

18 June 1942 James Paul McCartney is born to Mary Patricia Mohin and James McCartney in Liverpool.

1942 Finally giving in to family pressure, Julia Lennon reluctantly agrees temporarily to turn over the care of her infant son to her sister Mimi and Mimi's husband, dairy farmer George Smith.

1942 Despairing of her globe-trotting husband, Alf, ever settling down, Julia finally ends their 'on-again-off-again' relationship. She is soon to meet and fall in love with congenial barman John Albert Dykins. Together they take a small flat in the then tatty Gateacre district of Liverpool.

25 February 1943 George Harold Harrison, the youngest child of Harry and Louise Harrison, is born at 12 Arnold Grove, Wavertree, Liverpool.

19 June 1945 Julia gives birth to her second child, Victoria Elizabeth, at the Salvation Army's Elmswood Infirmary in North Mossley Hill Road, Liverpool. The father is not listed on the birth certificate, but was thought to be an army gunnery officer. The infant girl was subsequently adopted and is believed to have been taken by her new parents to Norway where today her ultimate fate still remains a mystery.

September 1945 Young John begins attending school at Dovedale Primary just around the corner from his aunt Mimi's home at 251 Menlove Avenue in Woolton.

July 1946 Alf returns from sea unexpectedly and convinces Mimi to allow John to accompany him on an impromptu holiday trek to Blackpool, secretly intending to spirit the boy away to a new life together in New Zealand. Luckily Julia locates the two and takes John back home to Liverpool.

5 March 1947 Julia Dykins, John Lennon's second sister and the first child of Julia and John Dykins, is born in Liverpool.

26 October 1949 Jacqui Gertrude Dykins is born in Liverpool.

September 1950 Young John Lennon is awarded a beginner's swimming certificate by the Liverpool Association of Schoolmasters.

July 1952 John leaves Dovedale Primary.

September 1952 John starts at Quarry Bank High School for boys.

5 June 1955 George Smith, Mimi's husband, dies unexpectedly of an undisclosed liver ailment at home, aged 52.

15 June 1956 Paul McCartney meets John Lennon for the first time at a Saturday afternoon performance by Lennon's schoolboy skiffle group, the Quarry Men, at St. Paul's parish fete in Woolton.

Shortly afterwards he is invited to join the group by Pete Shotton, a mutual friend of John and Paul (as well as being the Quarry Men's erstwhile washtub player).

September 1957 Cynthia Powell, aged 18, enrolls as a lettering student at the Liverpool Junior Art School. She soon transfers to Liverpool Art College where she first meets her future husband, fellow student John Lennon.

6 February 1958 Crackerjack guitarist George Harrison joins the Quarry Men. The nucleus of what would later be known as the Beatles is now formed.

Spring 1958 His Holiness the Maharishi Mahesh Yogi arrives in Hawaii to begin propagating his Transcendental Meditation Movement in the West.

15 July 1958 Julia Lennon, John's mother, is knocked down and killed by an off-duty police officer suspected of drinking, just outside Mimi's home on Menlove Avenue. John and his sisters are at home with John Dykins, playing outside. Julia's final words to Mimi just before the accident were, 'Don't worry.'

December 1958 John and Paul perform a few gigs together as The Nurk Twins.

29 August 1959 The Quarry Men are invited to play at the opening-night party of the Casbah, a teenage coffee club run by Mona Best, Pete's fun-loving mother.

15 November 1959 Renamed Johnny and the Moondogs, the band fails an audition for Carrol Levis at the Manchester Hippodrome.

5 May 1960 The flagging group, renamed once again as the Silver Beatles, fails another big audition to back singer Billy Fury. They are, however, chosen to tour with another young crooner, Johnny Gentle, on an upcoming trek through Scotland.

August 1960 Paul McCartney invites Pete Best to join the Beatles as their regular drummer on their first trip to Germany.

Autumn 1960 The Beatles make their first professional recording with members of their rival Liverpool group, Rory Storm and the Hurricanes, at Akustik Studios in Hamburg.

5 December 1960 The Beatles' trek to Germany is interrupted after George is found to be under-age by German immigration officials and is unceremoniously deported. The other Beatles soon follow and end up back in Liverpool, feeling beaten and dejected.

21 March 1961 The Beatles appear at the Cavern for the very first time. Over the next two years they will play there 292 times.

1 October 1961 John and Paul take off on a two-week hitch-hiking trip to Paris.

9 November 1961 Wealthy Liverpool record-retailer Brian Epstein unexpectedly drops in to the Cavern to hear the Beatles after being deluged with requests for their first official record release, 'My Bonnie' (a German Polydor import).

3 December 1961 Epstein invites the group to his office to discuss the possibility of taking them over as their manager.

1 January 1962 The Beatles travel down to London to audition for Decca Records. Despite a rousing performance by the Fabs, they were ultimately turned down by Decca bigwig Rick Rowe who ironically told Brian that groups with guitars are on the way out.

10 April 1962 Stuart Sutcliffe tragically dies of a brain haemorrhage in Hamburg. He was just 21 years old.

9 May 1962 The Beatles are offered a recording contract with Parlophone Records, a tiny offshoot of the vast EMI entertainment empire. Their recording manager is the brilliant George Martin.

16 August 1962 For reasons that remain a mystery even to this day, drummer Pete Best is unceremoniously sacked from the group and Ringo Starr is quickly brought in to fill the gap.

23 August 1962 John Lennon marries Cynthia Powell in a civil ceremony at the Mount Pleasant Register Office in Liverpool. Fellow Beatles, Harrison and McCartney attend.

5 October 1962 The single 'Love Me Do' is released.

31 December 1962 The Beatles make their final club appearance in Hamburg.

2 March 1963 'Please Please Me' hits the coveted number one position on the Melody Maker chart.

8 April 1963 John Charles Julian Lennon is born to John and Cynthia at 6.50 a.m. at Sefton General Hospital in Liverpool.

1 February 1964 'I Want To Hold Your Hand' is the number one record in America.

9 February 1964 The Beatles appear on The Ed Sullivan Show in New York. During their performance an estimated 73 million television viewers experience John, Paul, George and Ringo for the very first time. Across America not a single solitary crime is committed by a teenager.

23 March 1964 John Lennon's first book, In His Own Write, is published. Almost overnight it becomes an international bestseller.

10 July 1964 A civic reception is held in Liverpool to honour its most famous sons; over 100,000 people attend. Among them are John's sisters Julia and Jacqui as well as most of Lennon's family.

15 February 1965 John Lennon finally passes his driving test (after driving illegally for years).

12 June 1965 Buckingham Palace announces that the Beatles will be awarded MBEs later that year.

24 June 1965 John's second book, A Spaniard in the Works, is published.

3 August 1965 John buys his aunt Mimi a lovely seaside bungalow in Poole, Dorset.

31 December 1965 Alf Lennon suddenly reappears on the scene,

this time to release his one and only record, 'That's My Life (My Love and My Home)'. Although initially it receives quite a lot of airplay, it is critically panned and sells poorly.

4 March 1966 John makes his infamous remark about the Beatles being more popular than Jesus Christ during an interview with British journalist and Beatle crony, Maureen Cleave.

31 July 1966 Radio stations across America join together in an adhoc ban on Beatle music as a direct result of John's controversial remarks on the decline of Christianity in the West. Over the next few weeks there are reports of record burnings and other protests by groups ranging from the Klu Klux Klan to the Daughters of the American Revolution. In the midst of this furor, John is persuaded by Brian Epstein publicly to recant his remarks in an effort to calm middle America's shattered faith in the Fabs.

29 August 1966 The Beatles give their final American concert at Candlestick Park in San Francisco.

9 November 1966 John meets Yoko Ono for the first time at a special preview showing of her one-woman conceptual art show, 'Unfinished Paintings and Objects,' at the Indica Gallery in London.

26 May 1967 Sgt. Pepper's Lonely Hearts Club Band is released just in time to kick off the infamous 'summer of love.'

24 August 1967 The Beatles and an entourage of girlfriends, wives and hangers-on attend an introductory lecture on Transcendental Meditation given by the Maharishi at the Hilton Hotel, London.

27 August 1967 While attending a special weekend meditation seminar held in Bangor, Wales, the Beatles receive word that Brian Epstein has been found dead in his London townhouse due to an unexplained overdose of drugs. The Maharishi attempts to comfort them by reminding them to try and 'be happy' and 'don't worry.'

5 January 1968 Alf Lennon and his 19-year-old fiancee Pauline Stone meet John to seek his blessing for their forthcoming marriage. John is not too happy about this unexpected romance but reluctantly gives the two of them his support.

16 February 1968 John, Cynthia, George and his wife Pattie join the Maharishi in Rishikesh, India, for an intensive two-month instructor's course in transcendental meditation. The rest of the Beatles' entourage arrives four days late.

12 April 1968 The Beatles leave the peaceful mountain ashram two weeks ahead of schedule after a nasty rumour circulates that the giggly Indian fakir attempted to compromise the virtue of fellow meditator Mia Farrow.

22 August 1968 Cynthia Lennon sues John for divorce, citing his alleged adultery with Yoko Ono as the cause.

18 October 1968 John and Yoko are busted for possessing 219 grains of hashish at their flat at 34 Montagu Square, London. A charge of obstructing justice is also brought against the couple who, according to old Liverpool chum Pete Shotton, had been warned of the impending bust beforehand.

25 October 1968 Word leaks to the press that Yoko is pregnant. John Lennon is reportedly the father.

8 November 1968 Cynthia Lennon is granted divorce from John in an uncontested suit brought before magistrates in London.

21 November 1968 Yoko suffers her first painful miscarriage. John remains constantly at her bedside at Queen Charlotte's Hospital in London, where he beds down next to her in a sleeping-bag for several days.

28 November 1968 John pleads guilty to unauthorised possession of cannabis at Marylebone Magistrates Court. A fine of £150 is imposed as well as court costs of 20 guineas. The obstruction of justice charges are dropped against both John and Yoko.

29 November 1968 John and Yoko's infamous Unfinished Music Number One: Two Virgins is released. The scandalous album cover depicts the free-spirited couple naked.

30 January 1969 The Beatles play their last public performance ever on the rooftop at Apple Studios. The impromptu gig is filmed for inclusion in the Beatles' eclectic cinematic swansong Let It Be.

2 February 1969 Yoko Ono is granted a divorce from her former husband, Anthony Cox.

20 March 1969 John and Yoko are married in a quiet civil ceremony on the island of Gibraltar.

26 May 1969 The Lennons fly to Montreal to hold an eight-day 'Bed In' at the Queen Elizabeth Hotel. While there they record the now-famous counter-culture anthem, 'Give Peace a Chance.

1 July 1969 While visiting John's Aunt Mater in Durness, Sutherland, Scotland, the Lennons and their children Julian and Kyoko are involved in a car accident in Golspie. Although no one is seriously injured, John requires seventeen stitches on his face and head. His son Julian is also treated for shock.

12 October 1969 Yoko miscarries yet another baby. This time, however, the pregnancy is sufficiently long for the child, a little boy, to be given the name John Ono Lennon; he is buried in a tiny white coffin somewhere outside London. Only John and Yoko attend the service.

10 April 1970 Paul McCartney publicly quits the Beatles.

31 December 1970 Paul brings suit against the other Beatles in an effort legally to dissolve the group.

3 September 1971 John and Yoko say goodbye to England forever and fly off to America to make their new home.

16 March 1972 The Lennons are served with a deportation notice from American immigration officials due to John's 1968 drug conviction in England.

18 September 1973 John and Yoko go their separate ways, John to Los Angeles while Yoko stays ensconced in their palatial seven-room Manhattan apartment. The couple have now been married for four years.

January 1975 John returns home to New York and is reunited with Yoko. 'The separation just didn't work out,' he tells the press.

19 June 1975 John files suit against former Attorney-General John Mitchell for what his lawyers call 'improper selective persecution' relating to the government's deportation proceedings.

23 September 1975 As Yoko is now pregnant once again, immigration officials temporarily halt their deportation proceedings against John on what they call 'humanitarian grounds.'

7 October 1975 The New York Supreme Court reverses the deportation order against Lennon by a two-to-one vote.

9 October 1975 Yoko gives birth to the Lennons' only child together, a 7-pound baby boy they name Sean Ono Taro Lennon.

5 January 1976 The Beatles' former road manager and friend, Mal Evans, is shot dead by police in Los Angeles following an incident whereby Evans allegedly pointed a gun at officers responding to a domestic disturbance call. John is said to be deeply disturbed by the tragedy.

1 April 1976 Alf Lennon dies of cancer at Brigton General Hospital. He was aged 63.

27 July 1976 John finally receives his 'Green Card' at an immigration hearing in New York. John's only comment to the press was, 'It's great to be legal again.'

9 October 1976 John's self-imposed 'retirement' from show business and so-called 'house-husband' period commences. 'From now on,' Lennon tells the press, 'my chief responsibility is my family.'

15 October 1979 John and Yoko contribute $1,000 to the New York City Police Department for the purchase of several bullet-proof vests for officers.

14 July 1980 John and Sean set sail on the 63-foot sloop Isis, bound for Bermuda and accompanied by a five-man crew. It is during this holiday that John finally begins composing once again.

4 August 1980 John and Yoko begin recording at the Hit Factory in New York for the first time in six years. The music culled from those session is later to form the albums Double Fantasy and Milk and Honey.

9 October 1980 John celebrates his 40th birthday with his son Sean, who is five on the same day.

17 November 1980 Double Fantasy is released worldwide.

5 December 1980 John and Yoko are interviewed on their 'comeback' by Rolling Stone in New York.

8 December 1980 In the late afternoon, on his way out of the Dakota Building in Manhattan, John Lennon stops to give an autograph to a young man from Hawaii named Mark David Chapman. The two are photographed together. At 10.49 p.m. Chapman steps out of the shadows and guns down John Ono Winston Lennon as he returns home from a recording session accompanied by his wife Yoko. The world mourns John's loss.